CW01669030

The Emma Press Anthology of Dance

Also from the Emma Press

Poetry anthologies

The Emma Press Anthology of Mildly Erotic Verse
A Poetic Primer for Love and Seduction: Naso was my Tutor
The Emma Press Anthology of Motherhood
The Emma Press Anthology of Fatherhood
Homesickness and Exile: Poems about Longing and Belonging
Best Friends Forever: Poems on Female Friendship
Campaign in Poetry: The Emma Press Anthology of Political Poems
The Emma Press Anthology of Age (Sept '15)

Poetry anthologies for children

Falling Out of the Sky: Poems about Myths and Monsters

The Emma Press Picks

The Flower and the Plough, by Rachel Piercey
The Emmores, by Richard O'Brien
The Held and the Lost, by Kristen Roberts
Captain Love and the Five Joaquins, by John Clegg

Poetry pamphlets

Ikhda, by Ikhda, by Ikhda Ayuning Maharsi
Raspberries for the Ferry, by Andrew Wynn Owen
The Dead Snail Diaries, by Jamie McGarry
Rivers Wanted, by Rachel Piercey
Oils, by Stephen Sexton
Myrtle, by Ruth Wiggins
If I Lay on my Back I Saw Nothing but Naked Women,
by Jacqueline Saphra

THE EMMA PRESS ANTHOLOGY OF

Dance

Edited by Rachel Piercey and Emma Wright

With poems from Stephanie Arsoska, Sophie F Baker, Dzifa Benson, Jane Burn, John Canfield, George David Clark, Geraldine Clarkson, James Coghill, Brian Docherty, Claire Dyer, Francine Elena, Flora de Falbe, Katherine Gallagher, Hilary Gilmore, Rebecca Goss, Jan Heritage, Sarah Hesketh, Emma-Jane Hughes, Emma Jeremy, Carla Jones, Melinda Kallasmae, Anna Kisby, Gill Learner, Emma Lee, Julie Maclean, Martin Malone, Felicity Maxwell, Paul McMenemy, Margot Myers, Richard O'Brien, Rachel Piercey, Wendy Pratt, Rosie Sandler, Jacqueline Saphra, Catherine Smith, Maria Taylor, Pam Thompson, Andrew Wynn Owen and Lana Faith Young. Illustrated by Emma Wright.

THE EMMA PRESS

THE EMMA PRESS

First published in Great Britain in 2015
by the Emma Press Ltd

Poems copyright © individual copyright holders 2015
Selection copyright © Rachel Piercey and Emma Wright 2015
Illustrations and introduction copyright © Emma Wright 2015

All rights reserved.

The right of Rachel Piercey and Emma Wright to be identified as the editors of this work has been asserted by them in accordance with the Copyright, Designs and Patents Act 1988.

ISBN 978-1-910139-15-8

A CIP catalogue record of this book is available from the British Library.

Printed and bound in Great Britain
by Jasprint, Washington.

theemmapress.com
queries@theemmapress.com

Contents

Introduction

Why do we dance? Why are we drawn to watch? What is it that elevates flesh and bone into displays of heartstopping beauty? Rachel Piercey (my co-editor) and I wanted to explore these questions in *The Emma Press Anthology of Dance* and to take a look at how dance permeates people's everyday lives.

The public place of dance is well-documented. We dance at parties, in clubs and in classes, and we watch it at the theatre and on television. It marks special occasions and offers both escapism and a sharp reminder of what it means to be alive. Dancing in public has a way of heightening, even catalysing social dynamics. Pam Thompson's 'At Sadlers Wells' and Felicity Maxwell's 'Volta' both capture the potential for high internal drama within the microcosm of a dancefloor or stage, while Paul McMenemy's 'Scottish Country Dancing' and Maria Taylor's 'Learning the Steps' recall the ritual awkwardness of school dance lessons.

Dancing in private, on the other hand, is less easily pinned down. When and why do we dance when we're on our own, or nearly on our own? Poems such as George David Clark's 'Lullaby with Succotash', Rebecca Goss's 'Loco Motion' and Jan Heritage's 'Recapitulation' reveal the private place of dance in bedrooms, kitchens and streets, touched with as much drama as anything you might see on stage. Meanwhile, Martin Malone's 'Mic-ing the Kit' and Jacqueline Saphra's 'My Grandmother's watch' show us a kind of dance on an even more intimate level, within the minutiae of routines.

When selecting the poems for this anthology, Rachel and I wanted to give a sense of how dance is present at every stage of human life – not just as a metaphor for mortality but as a real, physical activity. From lessons to courtships to celebrations and moments when music just demands a response, dance is an essential part of our textured existence. We hope this book manages to express some of the joy and excitement of dancing, and that it might inspire some toe-tapping, swooping and swaying too.

Emma Wright
WINNERSH
April 2015

The Emma Press Anthology of Dance

Ginger Takes the Floor

Yes, I will dance,
my belly proud and paunchy
like a bag of ripe apples rolling
at the bottom of a barrel.
I will shake fields of flesh,
let folds ripple like rivers,
marching
unstoppable
down the mountain.
These thighs will shake with no shame,
arms held high like fat flags
waving my refusal to be hoisted
out of reach. I will let sweat
weave hot salt
down aubergine cheeks,
breasts jigging
with the rest of my jelly.
I am my own Ginger, no iced eye
will stop me spicing up this floor.

Lullaby with Succotash

maybe start talking say I like those
dangly things on your ears they're called earrings
I know that and while you're talking get out a bowl
and start peeling oranges to your lady say
can you do the succotash? and if yes do the succotash
with her a couple laps around the kitchen
with one hand on the small of her back and the other hand
still peeling oranges add key lime custard
and cherries and chocolate chips and syrup
are we making a doozie? tell her yes to a doozie
and smile why are you smiling? say just the way
you do the succotash with your hips and your eyes
going half the way through me pour in banana pudding
and clear tequila you'll make me dizzy I know that
you'll make me naked I know that
turn on the radio shake a little music
out of the speaker right into the bowl maybe
stop talking maybe kiss her neck and stir
let her taste a spoonful and if it needs a pinch of cinnamon
that's why we have spices take the dangly things
off her ears they're called earrings I know that
put the earrings in the bowl say your skin baby
say your lips say your sugar baby say taste it again
and if she thinks it's ready say let's eat it in bed

FELICITY MAXWELL

Volta

The Queen and Leicester dance again tonight.
I watch their tripping progress and their poised
flirtation, her ascension and his joy
to have his hands upon her as by right.
For me, I stand demure, with eyes not quite
cast down but certainly not bold to claim
the glance or hand of any lord. My aim
is low, and yet he finds me in his sight.
I turn. The court turns round about me –
its sudden centre – pivoting gossip
as my Lord of Leicester leads me round the hall.
Is not man's favour fickle? How can he
not deem it a most foolish thing to slip
from measured steps and, plunging, hazard all?

Irish Dancing on New Year's Eve

We were pissed, both staggering
among New Year's Eve gatherings,
heading out
on the stout
in the middle of town. Half swimming, half drowned
in the sweaty commotion and flailing for ground
in our three legged race.
Then a sound we could taste
poured over our heads. We rolled to a stop
at the foot of The Scholar, fell inside, claimed our lot
hand in hand by the door,
got the barman to pour
more booze than was wise. And we grinned
at each other; two ship-wrecked lovers, with gin
on our breaths,
hearts stretching our chests,
we danced like two loons, knocking tables
right over, chairs diving for cover; the rebels
of Guinness;
our business
each other. They asked us to leave
so we danced in the street
in the snow
and tomorrow:
a clean start to the year, clean hearts and clean heads
and no dates on the calendar yet circled in red.

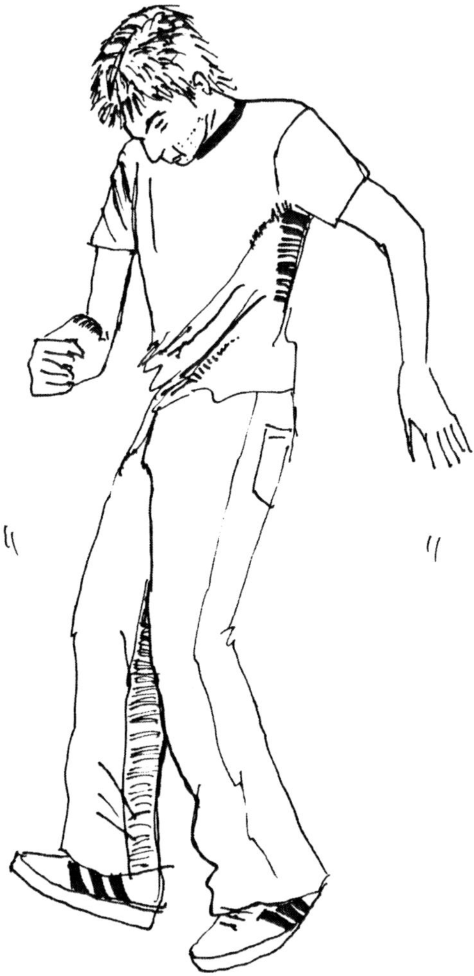

His Sister's Version

(after 'The Dance', a painting by Paula Rego)

Eight days after Mumping Day the moon was high
and white. The clouds had gone. The dance began. Feet,
tentative at first, stamped shadows
down, fixed them onto sand. There were nine
of us then; my famous brother in working clothes stood out.
His forearms gleamed. She couldn't get close

enough in that dress, stiff as a bell. Close
friend of his? Overlapping underskirts, mushroom taint;
a high smell stung me. Was it her or a tang of herring?
Out at sea, fishers staring at nothing. Feet
followed feet. Hers were lumpen, heavy. Nine
glasses upturned, not yet sea-filled, shadows

of wine still in them. Shadows?
I imagined him in a bright lane close
to the family he wanted. Yes, we were nine
when the dance began. Who could properly describe it? High
tide might have lashed us. That young girl's feet
were probably the sorest, so dervish-like she span. Called out

More, more and if her mother or grandmother lapsed out
of time she'd shake their hands like reins. Shadows
in our hallway always scared him. She danced on alone.
My feet, half the size of hers, tripped knowingly and light, close
to the cow cry inside her. How high
the moon now? Shrunken eye. Tense amoral pearl. Nine

beds with sheets turned back, abandoned; nine
mirrors ghosting smirks and scowls. Out
of the nine of us I knew he'd be the first. High
dive from the Plutonic Rocks, shadows
grappling at his clothes piled up like a cairn. Close
by, a note? A birthday card? To himself? Feet

away, the dancers still trod the sand. Feet
away, me in classiest yellow steadying a mannequin. Nine
feet away, or more now, she'd stopped dancing, was close
to the water, kicking off shoes, striding in. Get out
of there. The mannequin released me to the shadows
dancing by themselves, to the high

point of your birthday, brother, when your feet tried out
land again. Nine lives. Or shadows
that close at the year's end, rising moon-high.

Scottish Country Dancing

An accordion strains through a speaker,
    mutton through mincer,
slops on the sprung floor we skip over, trying not
to sticky up our sandshoes, scuffed white sergeants
dashing off the wallbars; gay as Gordons,
we step in to strip the willow, tying knots
in notional osiers and ourselves; each dancer

dodgems down the aisle, slaloms and slings
        – pachinko balls in six-eight time.
It was the closest dancing came to the fling
        and hurl of shinty, or those games
the teachers prised us out of; a joyful thing
we hadn't known existed stripped of shame.

My mother as horse

> I knew exactly and intimately how to be a horse: how it felt to have four legs, hooves and a tail, and would shape-shift for days on end... I have a sense that shape-shifting, as a state of mind, has a great deal in common with empathy, in that it allows you to become the person, animal or object of your concentration and for a few moments, understand how it feels to be inside that skin. The embodied metaphor in fact.
>
> – From 'Fairy Stories and the Use of Metaphor in Counselling', by Kath Baker

Puffs her chest when you try to saddle her,
A sharp kick – no surprise there.
Puts all her weight behind her way out, her way in,
No refusing celebration whatever the win.
A flank as smooth as any with a muscular curve,
Unbridled: hard to catch. Happier in a herd.
Her hair a disobedience in the bright Scottish wind,
Shuts her eyes to music, and for ballads, leans in.
Prefers the food of occasion to the everyday meal,
Loves to dance with that silver-shod flick of the heel.
Caprioles over waves in the storm-churned sea,
Takes risks now she knows what it is to be free.
A beast to break hearts, she is no sooner here,
Than a horse-shaped hole in the atmosphere.

Trevithick Day Dance

A steamrolled strip of tarmac tracks
a route straight through the town;
no traffic bothers it today,
instead, it is an aisle

for heel and toe to tread
in steps so synchronised

I've often wondered how they do not shake
Trevithick's statue to the ground.

*

Behind the brass band's looping tune
a trail of children, three
abreast, of bashful boys who stand
between two girls and clutch

the hands of both, move forward,
back, then forward, wearing

matching sashes and retracing steps
they studied all last week at school.

*

The grown-ups follow, marginally
more confident in steps
designed to be as mechanised
as that old Puffing Devil:

men come to a halt,
women spiral out,

the horses stood still, the wheels went around,
going up Camborne Hill, coming down.

*

Spectators line the street to watch
this train of dancers move
past pub and church and pub and church
to closed-shop bordered end,

led by the replicated
engine steam which now

conducts the annual dance, and yet on every
other day the wheels are still.

Festival Season (Strasbourg, 1518)

We didn't want to. Blame the government,
their agents in the streets with pipes and drums,
or better yet the weather, or whichever changes faster.
Blame the rain, the hail, the hunger;

it can't be no one, nothing that's behind this
cockroach limb-twitch, how our eyes roll round
like croutons soaked in soup and when you ask
our names we spit in tongues of fire.

If you don't believe me, taste my blood;
syringe my data as the speakers thud and scream
like children trapped in wells. My crops are dead,
my iron's low and I'll test positive for anything

except the Eucharist, and if those lights don't stop
some second soon the bulb inside my chest
will blow its fuse and smash. Hysteria:
we ate the things we ate *ergo* it's happening

because we asked it to, we brought it on ourselves
and brought it to the fields and the festivals
and drilled it underground in lightless rooms
in sunglasses and fake fur coats. Our bones are shivering

like houses made of matchsticks in a coastal wind.
I heard that once they did this to escape.
Escape from what, if not the blood churning
and the skin burning and my face wet

as a piñataed bladder? Now it spreads by sight,
it only takes one look and then your wrists snap
upwards and your knees say no to everything
they're told, your hips become a wave machine

you can't turn off, and if you think that it sounds funny
then it's not and you should try it. I am on the pulpit
frothing liturgies while my skeleton tries to step
sideways out of my skin. I run like a crab and my neck

is a spinning top. It's a matter of moments till my head
comes off. So let's hold hands and pray
or break each other's fingers if we have to
and let's clamp our tongues like traffic wardens,

try to take a breath that doesn't shoot blue sparks,
and failing that put glowsticks round our collarbones
and weave the catgut into crowns and jump.
We didn't want to dance. I told you once.

*

Author's Note: Strasbourg in 1518 saw the most extensive example of a puzzling medieval phenomenon: the dancing plague. Apparently believing themselves to be cursed, around 400 of the town's citizens felt an uncontrollable impulse to dance; the epidemic lasted for a month, and many died of exhaustion. The situation was not helped by the local authorities, who paid musicians to keep the dancers moving in order to purge their afflicted blood. Many theories have been proposed to explain these events; John Waller's book on the subject *A Time to Dance, A Time to Die* concludes that the 'plague' was an instance of mass psychogenic illness.

On Sand

They'd booked an umbrella sky,
her shoelessness a prelude,
the tide on the cusp.

He says the sea birds are not watching.
She says their other selves are icebergs,
dancing as icebergs do.

I say whoever's playing the soundtrack
must be on the pier built where the picture ends,
that when they waltz her skin's a shade of calico.

The fishing boats aren't yet back,
nets plump with the day's last catch.

A man on the quay is whistling
as he shuts the shutters of his shop.

Orcadian Strip the Willow, Hogmanay

When our turn comes at the chords –
their familiar crest, the sea outside,
making crescendos
in the final hours of December –
we knit, feet blunt,
to pull a circle against gravity.
The fiddle strings, restless girls
meeting you, leaving you, then again.
I am passed between strong hooks of arms,
men who have seen me all these years,
who send me back to you.
You leave, return and
we move as bees returned to the hive.
An unbuttoning then hot buttoning,
the accordion a weatherbeaten grin.
We are clumps of snow dissolving in a river,
breaking from our selves in blurs of family colour.
This aurora borealis from a Viking archipelago.
The moment a whoop flies out of a woman,
you might see bogle faces at the window.

Ballerina of the Night-Pool

I tried to write a poem last night
on the ballerina of the night-pool
who appeared, suddenly,
in my bed. There she was,
arms and legs akimbo, floating,
all poised beneath the covers in the dark –
and I couldn't do it.

In vain I wrestled sleep,
and tick-tocked the lamp to capture her,
elusive as her mermaid kin
yet resolutely legged and dancing:
a stork of grace with one knee raised in worship,
spiralling on a liquid stage.

All the cosmos of the water was there,
clear as night; its black infinities,
star-rippled surface, cool silken gliding
of currents and dreams and her thighs
as she floated, smiling,
amongst silences and tides of sheets,
a statue drowned mid-pirouette.

All the reedy smell of night was there,
overwhelming, when I lay down.
But up, with light and scratching pen,
it was impossible.
Off the details darted and she with them,
though I could feel her in the pause of
every limb's exalting ode.

We played chase for an hour until
I dropped off, cursing blind dull fingers,
while she minnowed away
to dance *pas de deux* with her reflections.

The corps

They want to dance Aurora
who unspools
dramatically to the floor

or Odette
who splits herself in two
or the great rift healer, Juliet.

But privately
the audience likes the corps
most of all, how they spring neatly,

parabola arms exactly
chalked onto the air.
Their careful matching

of dresses, legs and inclined
necks fits into
the rhythm of the body inside,

half known and half felt:
the precise, unfurling
geometry of cells.

We recognise
the arc of the two-headed coin
in their eyes –

the acute longing
to be set apart,
the charm of belonging.

Breathing underwater

My ballet teacher said
I had feet like kippers

so I took my fish-feet
to special classes, where

they grew strong, supple
and proud. We learned

to ignore the pinched-nose
protestations of the anti-fish

brigade: they'd never
witness the full-bellied

waltz of waves at high
tide or the polka beat

of rollers against rock.
Tired of being fish out

of water, my feet grew gills.
Now, they take me out at night:

samba across stony beach
to sea's edge; quick-step

through shallows; jive across
currents of sunshine-shoals;

salsa in the caress of ocean's
swell. Homebound, they

pirouette among stars'
reflections, sleek and

streamlined as a pair
of satin pointe shoes.

My Dancers

I drew them everywhere, not just
in sketchbooks; on brown envelopes
and letters home from school,
in the margins of my English book
– *Today's date is, on Saturday I...*
they leapt, in their leotards and tights,
on endless legs and insteps
arched high enough, in their silk shoes,
to make a principal ballerina weep.
I gave them angled heads, sleek necks,
a hard, knotted bun at each nape;
they arabesqued and pirouetted
through pencilled lists of times tables –
six sixes are thirty six – who cares? –
my dancers flew over the squared paper.
And sometimes I coloured them in –
gave them candyfloss skirts, black hair,
blue hair bands, ruby lips. Their eyes
glittered hectically from their exertions.
They got me into so much trouble,
my dancers – *Will you STOP drawing*
on your books, lose a merit mark,
a bright girl like you should know better...
I wanted to dance them away from the teacher,
from the chalk dust, glue, the morning tapes
of Elgar or Shostakovich they played
to civilise us – it wasn't Swan Lake,
my classmates were lumpen and wrong.
I wanted to take the tips of my dancers' fingers,
dance with them through the door
down the dull corridor, and out of my life.

At Sadlers Wells

After Matthew Bourne's *Swan Lake*

In Act 2, the royal bed becomes a cast-iron cot,
heraldic banners replaced by stark white blocks
because the queen in Dior
insists her son must wed the girl in the pink-
tasselled skirt even though the male swan's his dream made flesh,
all bare chest and feathered haunches

and this takes me back
to Christmas trees I saw on the way, in a jewellers
in the Burlington Arcade, trees of white feathers,
the walk down a red carpet, knowing that
for all I kept gazing, windows screened me from
what I'd never have

like in the final scene when the swans bowed their necks,
and the Stranger wrestled the Prince in a closing *pas de deux*,
there was no way out of an ending
where swans departed under a glassy moon
and courtiers shut palace doors to keep out the cold.

Dansmuseet

Not that I would have wanted it to be,
or last much longer than its natural term;
this is where it became
the stapling of motion on a sheet,
the crucifixion of ball-change and turn.

Like wings hanging from coat-hooks on the wall,
the gauze and masks, the figures caught en pointe
are braced like catgut strings –
somewhere between still lifes and wind-up dolls,
shins taut to catapult into the void.

This is, of course, an arbitrary point:
we'd wound ourselves up into arabesques,
but when I held the thread
and snipped it, it was senseless to recoil.
The flower doesn't choose when to be pressed:

I can't retrace one step, and if I could,
I wouldn't. This is how it works:
one foot moves first,
the other follows, trusting that what's good
cannot at once be spinning and preserved.

Music for the Brain

CLAP CLAP CLAP
why are we? CLAP
CLAP *COME ON!*
PACK UP YOUR TROUBLES
IN YOUR

mum hated that one
the rude brush it pulled it
howled through my hair
thank God your dad
was a protected trade CLAP

now the jive she'd say
that's a small person's dance
his hands CLAP *and*
CLAP *my hands*
the whole bruising
heartstart of it

Dancing on the Farm

I wanted to dance with my father,
dance fast over dirt tracks,
dance full-flight across creeks,
breeze past the watching crows,
surprise every sheep and cow –

jazz – waltz – foxtrot – jive –
to find some *joie-de-vivre*
that seemed to pass him by.

At my first bush dance,
he pulled me to my feet, saved me
from being a wallflower:
his way to say *caring.*

He was master of the slow waltz:
I'd seen his cool toe-balancing,
the grace of it, guiding my mother
into circles of Lehar and Strauss.
But the foxtrot…
Too fast, he shrugged, *I'm past it.*

I didn't believe him, standing there on the edge
of my dream with his face slightly pained,
as if giving bad news,
and the gentle side of him spoke:
a look that said he was vulnerable,

my Dad, opened up,
the weight of days holding his feet
to the boards.

Remembering Steps

I've seen you lunchtimes
plucking at your napkin,
picking up, peering at

and shifting salt and pepper.
Whose? you say.
Your lips, querulous,

searching for sipper cup spouts,
are certain today –
crooning and kissing.

Slippered feet are surer, too;
they remember the way
of a slow dance.

You hold a beloved; breathe
a near-forgotten song
soft upon a wee deaf ear;

and step closer to greet
the man on-screen
– who sings. You would

interrupt to introduce your babe
but find her tuckered out.
Naptime's familiar; you smile

and attempt to tuck her
atop magazines beside the TV.
Funny how things come back

and others don't.
You fuss, finesse, and recollect
how tricky settling a baby can be

when Lynn (in pinny)
waltzes up, arms open to take
your doll. She sways a moment

with her; gently
lays her upon the stack
of famous faces (out to lunch);

and – one-two-three,
one-two-three – offers
her arm and the lead.

The Dance

Hello. I am Frida.
That is all you need to know.
I am your personal future.
I will wash away your past.
I do not care how old you are,
whether you can make children.
You are now, I am now,
these pearls are now.
Let me pass the hat round.

But first, let me sing; I know
you will not let me dance,
although I could tell you
a story about your grandma
as a young woman, what her
sisters did in the caves,
out of the sight of men.

You should allow space
for dancing, for the things
your grandda never spoke
to you about. Listen to him
now, let him tell you why
he always wore a red hat.

How did he get that hat,
what did he do to achieve
his position, what did
grandma do to help him?
When you know these things,
come and find me. Do not
delay too long, the dance
goes on, with or without you.

Poppy Red, Lime Green

After 'Room in New York' by Edward Hopper

Her dress is the same colour as his chair
and the lampshade beside the upright piano
where she sits, finger cooling on an ivory key.
Her hair scraped back into a bun at her nape.
Her face in shadow as she looks down.

He sits in an armchair the same colour
as his wife's dress, the same colour
as the shade for the light not yet needed.
He wears a uniform suit and reads the paper,
not bothered by the music his wife may play.

The burst of citrus paint on the walls:
her inspiration for when she clears the furniture
and stamps out a flamenco after he's left for work,
still wondering why his wife's bloom is fading.

The dancers on graves

gather at dawn, 21st June, by the large yew;
limber up, leaning on the back ends of monuments
and tombs; adjust bandeaux and legwarmers;
yodel a little, do scales to loosen the chi.

The relevant areas are corralled with ribbon,
beginning with John Henry Frayn, *father of three*, down to
Dawn Mary Highgate, *a friend to all.*
The usual routines, salsa, merengue, rain-dance,

always come out altered on grass, especially
if the going is soft. Some were children when they
started; they say the day fits seamless
into their year. And a lady of ninety (who never forgot

the man who wronged her at seventeen),
resplendent in furs, performs a perfect foxtrot.
The Mercy Brigade, sitting to one side, allocate
marks for flirtatiousness, precision, grace.

L'Etoile

Tossed
like a shuttlecock

between
two black-suits

into the white light
it's always a bit of a blur

till rhythms
merge

to point
each feathered pirouette

backstage
the man

trousers his profit
loses his head

mine held firm
I like your wit M. Degas

you've captured that
perfectly but

the thump thump thump
of my heart

escapes you
both

Dance Instructor

Look at him lilting his shy feet
like a scared wren.
Some men!
He seems fairy fed.

You would think he could manage
a grasshopper's hello, but no.
He is no red-beaked cob.
No leaping neck that
surges forward, honking and pecking.

He is almost without wings.
Such a delicate performance may
be pinched off
by a schoolboy's taunt.

There is the danger, with a type
such as this, that meeting
a young girl's gaze may spill him
into dizzying twirls
that wrap him into a warm night shadow.
Oh, but don't come complaining
when there is nothing you can do
to reach him through his cocoon of mad romance.

Still, if you're sure you want him for a lover
I'm sure
I can rustle up some gauze to pad
out your thin hips. And I have lipstick
to brighten your dry mouth.

Oh! But look who's shuffling over!
You might try the cabriole, if he's so shy, see if you can't bring out his inner tiger.

The One Where I Sleep Next to You

Sometimes, when I dream, you are talking
to the projection of a dancing woman
on the wall of our bedroom. Her outline
quivers as she dances like a flat Ginger Rogers.
You are asking her questions like –
If I tied a million coins to a million
balloons, and let them all float down
to the homeless in London, would I feel
better about myself? – and other things
that don't make sense. Sometimes
she answers your questions with a yes
or a no. This time she holds up
her shaking palms and looks at you
with a barely-there face before her
outline shatters, falling like expensive
looking rain onto the floor where the
light soaks in and disappears.

Munch was Probably a Terrible Dancer

I was still in bed when you called.
You asked about my mood
and I replied: *amphibious*
then slithered out onto the floor
as you hung up
into a small, horrible puddle of *me*.

Today I am droving myself to an art gallery
in Oslo. It's a hard life, but I will try
to enjoy it: all the people I do not care for,
all the things I do not want.

Arriving there, as if by accident,
I decide to start with the painting I like the least:
The Dance of Life, an allegory
for the way fate foxtrots on our bones,
leaving us strong and sallow,
face deep in our allotted partners – the one

on the right hand especially, to the left
of the widow with sorrow
analogous to the maiden at the start
of the picture

with the stamen thrust of a rose coming at her
and the moon dreary and stranded
on its own self-shone pedestal.

I try not to think too much.
But I think of clubs. Think of hips
engulfed in hands and arms,

grinding and daggering –
the Paolo and Francesca in the corner,
aloof from it all in the goblet
of their mutual breath.

And Munch was scared of many things.
He looked at them, hard. He was probably
scared of dance, that stately
orchestration of the two into one,
courtly and chaotic spectacle
spun along that knife edge between release
and restraint.

Alligator Pear

a sad story on the menu again
I tell her   eat the avocado

get past its pebbly skin
the calloused hands of your
grandfather gripping your waist
the white dress with the
primrose trim   go for the soft

interior   mild, good for a crisp
fried soul in need of a salsa

good on a piece of toast   oily as
the tango man with yellowing teeth

keeping away the squamous cells
that dance into your night

clasping you like a dark faux lover
just as hungry

A Brief Index

(in the ways in which you make my heart dance)

1) My heart, for you, is full of fat spirals
and long tender pirouettes

2) It tremors the sultry sway
of extreme heatwaves
at the crease of your uncertain mouth

3) It spins on its head and backflips
as if all these years haven't even passed through it
when you look at me
that way

4) And when you move close enough to touch
it hops, counting and holding its pathetic breath
praying it won't tread too heavily
sweat
or break entirely

5) But at your kiss it roars
a furious beast in full charge

galloping about
a charming Paso Doble

How I Learned to Dance with the Octopus

He whispered in the slipstream:
Shake what your mama gave you
wind your body, wiggle your jelly
this is no time to minnow around.

Keen to divine time and tide, I smeared
brine at my pulse points, spritzed fish sauce
under my arms. The itching set in – my skin,
scaly in dusk's mauve light, began to sheen.

Swaying to the cadence of underwater waves
I dived, careful not to splash, into the big,
billowing blue. It was tricky seeking
a beastie gowned in glamours of rock,
coconut, cuttlefish, nautilus...

I waited –

resolve locked down to the rock-steady beat
of my iridescent tail fin. At dawn, I emptied
my lungs, flexed my new gills, my aura
floated free, morphed into sepia. Behind
the inky nimbus lurked the king of camouflage,
my crepuscular hunter.

One arm fed through, copped a feel, took
the weight of my breast in the curve
of a lissom limb, measured the rhythm
of my heart like a stethoscope. One sucked

my neck gently, branded his hickey, plugged
my navel, probed my mantle cavity. A muscular curl
furled my fused legs, held my tail down –
I was no longer bipedal. Tickling my shell
with the last of his tentacles he drawled:

I am Wunderpus Photogenicus.
You're ready. Keep it steady. Let's waltz.

Mic-ing the Kit

'Here space is everything, for time ceases to quicken memory.' – Gaston Bachelard

My favourite hour of any session was
mic-ing the kit. Beyer, Electrovoice,
Neumann, Sennhauser, AKG and Shure;
sensitive diaphragms, phantom power.

This was analogue, unsampled and raw,
the real business of capturing sound:
the cottage loaf of pressure gradients,
the sideways heart of cardioid response.

Often, I would send away the drummer,
ply him with tea or weed to leave me there
– free of his twitches and random hits –
alone with his kit, sexing it in space.

There were the routine no-brainers, holy
trinities and givens: bass drum, hi-hat
and snare meant the egg of the D-twelve,
C-four-one-four, SM fifty-seven.

There was the metalwork and toms, beloved
of drummers, loathed by myself. I always
did my best by them: stringing up condensers,
top mic-ing the mounted mids, crash and ride.

Then things got interesting in the room
with your own little signatures or tricks.
A woodcutter now, you knew the grain
of the space; its sweet spots and hard-knots.

The snare's true *logos* was to be had reflected
from some wall or favourite corner; its kingfisher
reverb caught fire in a Gents' urinal,
where the porcelain gave sympathetic decay.

Making my way back to the control room
through the vineyard of leads, through the heavy
anechoic doors, I was usually happy.
Artisan's work: preparing the dance.

Live Love Long

on Monday nights pale grey men
hold me tight to demonstrate
the ins and outs of the
cha cha cha

on Tuesday I plant banksia
integrifolia to lure the trembling
spinebill to new nectar in the
neighbourhood

(by the way) the snail has a brain
is a bit of a Don Juan when it comes to love
sleeps through the cold   drought
or flood   could be your
teenage son   then Venus all eyes
sees lovers entwine super-coiled in courtship
before the love dart shoots home

then they smoke a
cigarette   go for a pee
just a story   random spiral
unravelling in a soft shoe shuffle
hip hop freestyle
a slow   slow   quick-quick   slow

Recapitulation

The man who lives above me
is a model neighbour
keeps no clutter in the communal ways
recycles the junk mail.
I like his eyes and much about him
but we are not exactly friends.
We stick to pleasantries.

Perhaps he knows I hear him
dancing late at night, moves imprinted
on my nearly sleep
so that I have learned each turn
each step ball change.
He is considerate
keeps the volume low.

But I wait for those deep E majors
I've Had... the Time of My Life...
The woman on the ground floor
who is best avoided
told me he was left standing
in a church porch, in a good suit
an orchid pinned to his lapel.

I lie still, try to detect
missed beats, but he is well-rehearsed
would not have put a foot wrong
allows enough space and weight
for an absent bride, inhales
at precisely the right moment
for that final lift.

Loco Motion

Said he was a painter,
that he'd always wanted to paint
the naked female form
hanging upside down.

We went to a hotel room.
I got a little crazy
on my first whisky,
started dancing,
making him do it too,
so we were turning
and shaking, both of us
naked
and screaming.

'D'you think you'd hang for me darlin'?'
We were on the floor, gasping
at the really high ceiling.
I turned my face towards him,
'Bet your life.'

Tea Dance Dresses

What am I thinking when I ask these things?
I saw us dancing like people did in the old days –
in the way no one would dance now,
unless they took a class.

The music laid in mosaic swirls, the stride of your thigh
between mine – back, side, together,
forward, side, together.
Spinning, the full parachute of my skirt unrolling
in pleats of albatross wing. Lips – post box red,
I am slim as bittern reeds.

The liquorice pinwheel curls around my head
leak setting-lotion whiff into the voltaic
air between our faces.

I ball my head beneath your ear so
I can smell the tender of your neck.
I do not know these steps but I would learn.
Where would I even go to hear such songs?

MARIA TAYLOR

Learning the Steps

Every Saturday, our dance teacher looks up
to God in the light bulbs and silently prays
our trainers will turn into red shoes. *Amen.*

We're not ballerinas. We're looping in circles
and getting nowhere, mostly anticlockwise,
making vines out of arms and legs.

We dance to learn about a part of ourselves
books can't teach; it's what our parents expect.
If we hop on a wrong note a bear will eat us.

We're learning the steps of old island lives:
hasapiko, kalamatiano, syrto; a dragging dance
where you're carried along by the wrists.

We leap like salmon, trying to catch scent of home,
as music pours through speakers like water
and our bodies vibrate with the boom.

Still, there we go again, tripping up,
making shoddy Xs with feet that want
to place themselves on an invisible map.

How Maisie Found Her Feet

It began in the hands – a pudgy pat-a-cake,
a spider's diamond climb. Next the hokey-cokey
and a waltz on Daddy's shoes. She bounced Teddy
to a picnic, held Bob's front paws and jiggled him
to Twelfth Street Rag. Best days at school brought
rainy lunch-times in the dining hall – they'd slide
and stamp with St Bernard and Paul Jones.
But ballet moved her not at all – her *entre-chats*
and *arabesques* were half a bar behind; tap
rattled her teeth, Isadora made her squirm.

When the telly started Dancing Club her heart
beat *quick-quick-slow*. She enrolled with Arthur Murray,
started stepping out with Ron and quite soon
her two left feet became a pair. They swept the floor
for thirty years in quickstep, samba, waltz,
before Ronnie popped his patent leather pumps.
She packed away her spangled shoes, the taffeta
and tulle, to sit out in a tango-less decline. Then
Strictly made her insteps itch and syncopations
flickered through her dreams. She braved
a tea-dance in the town and now fishtails, whisks
and chassés with the swinging Evergreens.

My Grandmother's watch

It was the wedding gift
that wound her up, the one
that lost five minutes a week.

Every quarter year, hostage
to the tick and itch,
she'd lace her town-wife boots,

arrange her fancy hat
and take a trip to where
the blinds were always lowered.

The watchmaker would grip
his loupe tight
in one muscled eye.

She'd stand in the magnified
depths of his gaze, pass
the watch across the counter.

With slow and absolute attention,
he'd turn it on its face,
ease it open, strip it down

to cog and wheel.
Beneath her peacock brim,
she'd watch him work.

In his hands, the silver pulse
would quicken, slipped hours
would re-align.

She'd dance a tango
in her mind, his troupe
of errant clocks beating time.

Afterwards, she'd trip home,
lighter, faster,
heart ticking with intent.

All those minutes regained:
she dreamed of squeezing them
back into the hollows

of those satin shoes she hadn't worn
for decades, the ones that meant
only that kind of dancing.

Le Corsaire

Look what the sea dragged in,
rugged and salt-cheeked like a bit of weathered glass.
All the ladies love a pirate. All the pirate loves
is the lady with limbs like fireworks,
throwing herself from shape to shape as though made of light.
If sold, she'll slip your fist before you touch her;
if bought, she'll call her pirate king to save her;
and storms will send them skipping over waves, unchained,
her hair still, somehow, full of flowers.

Dance in a Round

My mother was trained in Ballet
and toured Europe, until I
bulged under her voile skirts,
in her seven-and-a-half stones.

So I boarded at a dance school
and learnt Modern; in pastel Lycra
I stepped lightly, ate sparingly;
only the dancing had progressed.

Now my seven-year-old daughter
springs across our wooden floor,
leaps the breadth of the lounge and lands
hard; strides to her room calling me.

I am conscious of her every step –
imagine it is me – remember
Girls! What a herd of elephants!
Something she will never hear.

I follow, instructed to watch her new
Street Dance moves, learned at class,
or copied from music videos,
freestyling in her bright, baggy clothes.

There is no heaviness here, only
definition and strength. Her smile
radiates light. The music is loud.
I don't hear the echo of her feet.

Syncopation

It's the fizz of the fuel, fixing the rush that thrills –
Measure, quickening motion, spills
Ankleticklish and wrongrighting as, cut-looser, you cut your dash
With a revel of toe, tripping to lightest sleights
Like the geysering oil ignites
Tugging closer the gridlocking, the far-flung when we'll all be ash.

Meantime, move and remove, trellis your tendril limbs
Like the river that laps and brims
Borderbounded and rock-lucky: this lockdown is the lot of sound
Which is wavy in flight, fractious for reaching ear.
Pulse-in-body's the puppeteer
Syncopating and time-trimmed on the hard-shoulder of shaken ground.

Grandmother was a Showgirl

She wore a skirt like a staircase so he climbed it, pawed
at the cabinet of her bosom when she twirled him.

He flicked her with his tiny tongue as they spun, slid down
the bannister of her hip and thigh.

Her gold court shoes were piano pedals going *oompah oompah!*
She wore the boy like an ankle-strap *o-me-o-mi!*

Any moment she might high-kick him into a sky where some big
hand was chalking aeroplane lines.

He could hear the two Marys over the fence, the notes jumping
pah pah pah out the back door, washing falling off the line.

His whole life he will never dance like this with any other dame,
never so held or so high.

When she sets him down two magpies, slick-suited, hop to him
and enquire *May we too come to the ball?*

The fuchsias jingle *fleur-de-li fleur-de-la!* and the world
won't stop spinning.

Acknowledgements

'Lullaby with Succotash', by George David Clark, was first published in *Salt Hill* 22 (2009).

'Irish Dancing on New Year's Eve', by Wendy Pratt, was first published in her collection *Museum Pieces* (Prolebooks, 2013).

'Orcadian Strip the Willow, Hogmanay', by Francine Elena, first appeared in *The Honest Ulsterman* in 2014.

'The Corps', by Rachel Piercey, first appeared in *Bedford Square 5* (Ward Wood Publishing, 2011).

'Music for the Brain', by Sarah Hesketh, was first published in her collection *The Hard Word Box* (Penned in the Margins, 2014).

'Dancing on the Farm', by Katherine Gallagher, was first published in her collection *Circus-Apprentice* (Arc, 2006).

'The dancers on graves', by Geraldine Clarkson, was first published in *The Rialto* 80 (Spring/Summer 2014).

'Alligator Pear', by Julie Maclean, was first published in her collection *When I Saw Jimi* (Indigo Dreams, 2013).

'Mic-ing the Kit', by Martin Malone, was first published in his first collection *The Waiting Hillside* (Templar, 2011).

'Live Love Long', by Julie Maclean, was a winner of the 2010 Australian Tango Poetry Competition and was published in her collection *When I Saw Jimi* (Indigo Dreams, 2013).

'Loco Motion', by Rebecca Goss, was first published in her collection *The Anatomy of Structures* (Flambard Press, 2010).

'Le Corsaire', by Flora de Falbe, won the Young Poets Network English National Ballet challenge and first appeared on the Young Poets Network and English National Ballet websites.

'Grandmother was a Showgirl', by Anna Kisby, was first published in *Mslexia* 64 (Winter 2014/15).

About the poets

Stephanie Arsoska has been published by the Emma Press, *Prole*, Iron Press, Mother's Milk Books, *Magma, Ink Sweat & Tears* and *Nutshells & Nuggets*. She was a finalist in the Stanza digital slam and featured on the IndieFeed Spoken Word podcast. She runs a Virtual Open Mic Night on her website stephaniearsoska.co.uk.

Sophie F Baker has been published in magazines including *Smiths Knoll, The Rialto, Poetry London* and *Magma*. She won an Andrew Waterhouse Award from New Writing North in 2010 and an Eric Gregory Award in 2012. She works at the Poetry Society and is a founding editor of poetry magazine *Butcher's Dog*.

Dzifa Benson was born in London to Ghanaian parents and grew up in west Africa. She writes, performs, curates and teaches, and has performed her work at venues including Tate Britain, the Institute of Contemporary Arts and the Southbank Centre. She was a writer in residence at the Courtauld Institute of Art in 2007-8.

Jane Burn is an artist and writer based in the North East. She is a member of many poetry groups and her work has been published in a variety of magazines. She likes to write about minutiae of everyday life: loss, success, failure, fantastical thoughts and the joy and peace of nature.

John Canfield grew up in Cornwall and now lives in London. His poems have appeared in magazines and anthologies including *Oxford Poetry* XIV.2, *Transom* Issue 5, *Newspaper Taxis* (Seren, 2013), *Coin Opera II* (Sidekick Books, 2013) and *The Emma Press Anthology of Fatherhood* (Emma Press, 2014).

George David Clark teaches creative writing and literature in the honors college at Valparaiso University. His first book, *Reveille* (University of Arkansas Press, 2015), won the Miller Williams Prize and his poems have been published widely. He is the editor of *32 Poems* and lives in Indiana with his wife and their three young children.

Geraldine Clarkson is based in Warwickshire. Her poems have appeared in *The Best British Poetry* (Salt, 2014), *The Rialto, The Poetry Review, Poetry London, Ambit, Iota* and *Under the Radar*. She was the Selected Poet in *Magma* 58 and won the Ware Sonnet Prize in 2014. She is currently working on her first collection.

James Coghill has been published in *Homesickness and Exile* (Emma Press, 2014), *Ink Sweat & Tears, Verse Kraken* and *Lighthouse Literary Journal*, with work forthcoming in *Astronaut* zine and *Birdbook 3* (Sidekick Books). He likes to dance, but is unfortunately terrible at it. He is currently teaching himself Swedish.

Flora de Falbe comes from London and is currently in her first year studying English at Cambridge. She won the Foyle Young Poets of the Year Award in 2011 and 2012 and took part in the 2014 Tower Poetry Summer School. She was recently published in *CAKE* journal and the Emma Press's *Motherhood* and *Fatherhood* anthologies.

Brian Docherty was born in Glasgow and now lives in north London. He has published three books: *Armchair Theatre* (Hearing Eye, 1999), *Desk with a View* (Hearing Eye, 2008) and *Woke up this Morning* (Smokestack Books, 2012), with a fourth, *Independence Day*, forthcoming from the Penniless Press.

Claire Dyer's poetry collection, *Eleven Rooms*, was published by Two Rivers Press in 2013. Her two novels, *The Moment* and *The Perfect Affair*, and her short story, *Falling for Gatsby*, are published by Quercus. She has an MA in Creative Writing from Royal Holloway, University of London.

Francine Elena was born in 1986 and grew up in London, Lisbon and Scotland. Her unpublished pamphlet *Fluoro* was shortlisted for the 2014 Pighog Prize and her poems have been published in *The Best British Poetry* (Salt, 2013), *Best Friends Forever* (Emma Press, 2014), *Poetry London, Ambit, 3:AM Magazine* and *The Quietus*.

Katherine Gallagher was born in Australia and has lived in north London since 1979. She has five full collections, most recently *Car-*

nival Edge: New & Selected Poems (Arc Publications, 2010), and she has won various awards including the Warana Prize, a Royal Literary Fund Bursary and a London Society of Authors' Foundation Award.

Hilary Gilmore lives between London and her native Blue Mountains in Sydney, after eleven years based in Britain and Eastern Europe. Her professional life concerns the histories and cultures of dress, and she is a Visiting Fellow at the University of Southampton. Her poetry has been published in *Motherhood* (Emma Press, 2014) and *Once Wild*, the 2014 Newcastle Poetry Prize Anthology.

Rebecca Goss grew up in Suffolk and returned to live there in 2013, having lived in Liverpool for twenty years. Her second collection, *Her Birth* (Carcanet/Northern House, 2013), was shortlisted for the 2013 Forward Prize for Best Collection. In 2014 she was selected as one of the Poetry Book Society's Next Generation Poets.

Jan Heritage has recently completed the Royal Holloway MA in Creative Writing and has had poems published in several magazines. Back in the day she was Faber's Promotions Manager. Now she teaches yoga in Brighton.

Sarah Hesketh has been published in magazines and anthologies including *The White Review, Catechism: Poems for Pussy Riot* and *Other Countries: Contemporary Poets Rewiring History*. Her second collection, *The Hard Word Box* (Penned in the Margins, 2014), was inspired by her time as poet in residence with Age Concern.

Emma-Jane Hughes was brought up between the sublime of a river barge and the ridiculous of boarding school. She has been published in two Bridport anthologies, online by *Mslexia*, and in other anthologies. Emma is researching and teaching at the University of Chichester, and remains indebted to the lecturers there.

Emma Jeremy was born in Bristol and is currently based in London, working towards an MA in Creative Writing. Her work has appeared in *Rising, Poems in Which, The Voices Inside Our Heads, Nutshell* and *Best Friends Forever* (Emma Press, 2014).

Carla Jones grew up in Surrey and now lives in Bedfordshire. Her poems have been published in *Iota* and *The New Writer.* When she's not writing, she compulsively cuts up paper and doodles on things.

Melinda Kallasmae's poems have most recently been published in *Best Australian Poems* (Black Inc. Publishing, 2014), *The Stars Like Sand: Australian Speculative Poetry* (Interactive Press, 2014), and *The Emma Press Anthology of Motherhood* (Emma Press, 2014). Once upon a time, Melinda enjoyed maypole dancing.

Anna Kisby is an archivist living in Brighton. Her poems have been placed in competitions and published in magazines and anthologies including *Magma, Mslexia, Poetry News, Ink Sweat & Tears* and *The Emma Press Anthology of Motherhood.* She won *The New Writer* magazine's single poem prize in 2011.

Gill Learner's poetry has won several awards and has been widely published, most recently in *The Interpreter's House* 56, *Agenda* 48 and *Her Wings of Glass* (Second Light Publications, 2014). Her first collection, *The Agister's Experiment,* was published by Two Rivers Press in 2011 and she hopes to have a second in 2016.

Emma Lee has published two collections – *Mimicking a Snowdrop* (Thynks Press, 2014) and *Yellow Torchlight and the Blues* (Original Plus, 2004) – and her third, *Ghosts in the Desert,* is forthcoming from Indigo Dreams Publishing in 2015. She blogs at http://emmalee1.wordpress.com and reviews for *London Grip* and *Sabotage Reviews.*

Julie Maclean is the author of *Kiss of the Viking* (Poetry Salzburg, 2014), *When I saw Jimi* (Indigo Dreams Publishing, 2013) and *You Love You Leave* (Kind of a Hurricane Press, 2014). She has been shortlisted for the Crashaw Prize (Salt) and was the joint winner of the Geoff Stevens Poetry Prize.

Martin Malone was born in County Durham and now lives in Warwickshire. His poems have been published in a number of magazines and he is currently studying for a PhD in poetry at Sheffield University. He edits *The Interpreter's House* poetry journal and his second collection, *Cur*, will be published by Shoestring Press in 2015.

Felicity Maxwell is a postdoctoral researcher on 'The Reception and Circulation of Early Modern Women's Writing, 1550-1700' project at the National University of Ireland, Galway. Her sonnets have appeared in *Goblin Fruit* and *Sonnetto Poesia*. Her sonnet in this book was inspired by her learning Elizabeth I's favourite dance.

Paul McMenemy is the editor of Lunar Poetry. He can't dance.

Margot Myers lives in Oxford and has been writing poems for three years. She is interested in the use of myth in poetry and is working on a series of poems about the park where she walks her dog every day. Several of her poems have been commended in poetry competitions.

Richard O'Brien's second pamphlet, *The Emmores*, was published by the Emma Press in January 2014 and *A Bloody Mess* followed from Valley Press later that year. His work has featured in *Poetry London*, *The Salt Book of Younger Poets* (Salt, 2011) and *The Best British Poetry* (Salt, 2013). He is working on a PhD in contemporary verse drama.

Wendy Pratt was born in Scarborough in 1978 and now lives just outside Filey. She recently completed a BA in English Literature with the Open University and is now studying towards her MA in creative writing with the MMU. Her second pamphlet, *Lapstrake*, will be published by Flarestack Poets in 2015.

Rosie Sandler lives in Essex with her husband and their two children. In this estuary spot, she writes suitably watery poems, as well as stories and novels. Her poetry has appeared in *The Rialto*, *The Poetry of Sex* (Penguin Books, 2014) and *London Grip* e-zine. She runs The Poet's Resource at https://thepoetsresource.wordpress.com/

Jacqueline Saphra teaches at The Poetry School. Her first full collection, *The Kitchen of Lovely Contraptions* (flipped eye, 2011), was nominated for the Aldeburgh First Collection Prize and an illustrated book of prose poems, *If I Lay On My Back I Saw Nothing But Naked Women*, was recently published by the Emma Press.

Two of **Catherine Smith**'s collections, *The New Bride* and *Lip* (both Smith/Doorstop, 2000 and 2008) have been shortlisted for Forward Prizes. Her poetry is widely anthologised and her latest pamphlet-length publication, *The New Cockaigne* (Frogmore Press, 2014), is a surreal, supernatural satire on revolution, excess and restraint.

Maria Taylor's poems have appeared in a variety of magazines, including *The Rialto, Magma, Stand* and *The North*. Her debut collection, *Melanchrini*, was published by Nine Arches Press in 2012 and shortlisted for the Michael Murphy Memorial Prize in 2013. She blogs at http://miskinataylor.blogspot.co.uk/

Pam Thompson is a poet and university lecturer based in Leicester. She is one of the organisers of Word!, a spoken-word night at The Y Theatre and her publications include *The Japan Quiz* (Redbeck Press, 2009) and *Show Date and Time* (Smith/Doorstop, 2006). She won First Prize (Judges' Prize) in the Magma Poetry Competition in 2015.

Andrew Wynn Owen studies English literature at Magdalen College, Oxford. His first pamphlet, *Raspberries for the Ferry*, was published by the Emma Press in 2014. Also in 2014, he was awarded Oxford University's Newdigate and Lord Alfred Douglas prizes for poetry.

Lana Faith Young lives in Tasmania and is currently studying Creative Writing and Screen Studies at Griffith University. In 2012, Lana was shortlisted for the Western Australian Premiere's Book Awards in the digital narrative category. Lana loves poetry, writing children's books and jumping ocean waves.

About the editors

Rachel Piercey is a former editor at *The Cadaverine* magazine and a current editor at the Emma Press. She studied English Literature at St Hugh's College, Oxford, where she won the Newdigate Prize in 2008. Her illustrated pamphlet of love poems, *The Flower and the Plough*, was published by the Emma Press in 2013 and her second pamphlet, *Rivers Wanted*, in 2014.

Emma Wright studied Classics at Brasenose College, Oxford. She worked in ebook production at Orion Publishing Group before leaving to set up the Emma Press in 2012. In 2013 she toured the UK with The Mildly Erotic Poetry Tour, supported with funding from Arts Council England as part of the Lottery-funded Grants for the arts programme.

The Emma Press

small press, big dreams

The Emma Press is an independent publisher dedicated to producing beautiful, thought-provoking books. It was founded in 2012 by Emma Wright in Winnersh, UK, and *The Flower and the Plough*, by Rachel Piercey, was our first publication. In 2014 the Press was shortlisted for the Michael Marks Award for poetry pamphlet publishers. We share a blog with Scarborough's Valley Press and can sometimes be spotted sharing a table at bookfairs and at each other's events.

Our current publishing programme features a mixture of themed poetry anthologies and single-author poetry and prose pamphlets, with an ongoing engagement with the works of the Roman poet Ovid. We publish books which excite us, and we are often on the lookout for new writing.

Sign up to the monthly Emma Press newsletter to hear about all our events and publications, as well as our upcoming calls for submissions. All of our books are available to buy from our online shop, as well as to order or buy from all good bookshops.

http://theemmapress.com
http://emmavalleypress.blogspot.co.uk/

Also from the Emma Press

HOMESICKNESS AND EXILE, *edited by Rachel Piercey and Emma Wright*

ISBN: 978 1 910139 02 8 – PRICE: £10 / $17

Twenty-eight modern poets expand on Ovid's themes in the *Tristia*, exploring spiritual as well as physical exile in the modern world.

THE DEAD SNAIL DIARIES, *by Jamie McGarry*

ISBN: 978 0 9574596 9 4 – PRICE: £8.50 / $15

A collection of observational poems and literary parodies about snail culture, as told by a prematurely-crushed snail poet.

BEST FRIENDS FOREVER, *edited by Amy Key*

ISBN: 978 1 910139 07 3 – PRICE: £10 / $17

A celebration of the transformative power of the frequently overlooked and misunderstood relationship that is female friendship.

OILS, *by Stephen Sexton*

ISBN: 978 1 910139 03 5 – PRICE: £6.50 / $12

Belfast poet Stephen Sexton evokes melancholy and a strange kind of romance in *Oils*, the PBS Winter Pamphlet Choice 2014.

IF I LAY ON MY BACK I SAW NOTHING BUT NAKED WOMEN, *by Jacqueline Saphra, illustrated by Mark Andrew Webber*

ISBN: 978 1 910139 06 6 – PRICE: £12.50 / $21

Saphra's prose poems describe the comings and goings of eccentric parents and step-parents from a child's point of view. Webber's full-colour linocut prints complement the eerie atmosphere beautifully.